DODD, MEAD WONDERS BOOKS

WONDERS OF ALLIGATORS AND CROCODILES by Wyatt Blassingame
WONDERS OF ANIMAL ARCHITECTURE by Sigmund A. Lavine
WONDERS OF ANIMAL NURSERIES by Jacquelyn Berrill
WONDERS OF BARNACLES by Arnold Ross and William K. Emerson
WONDERS OF THE BAT WORLD by Sigmund A. Lavine
WONDERS BEYOND THE SOLAR SYSTEM by Rocco Feravolo
WONDERS OF THE BISON WORLD by Sigmund A. Lavine and Vincent Scuro
WONDERS OF THE CACTUS WORLD by Sigmund A. Lavine
WONDERS OF CARIBOU by Jim Rearden
WONDERS OF THE DINOSAUR WORLD by William H. Matthews III
WONDERS OF THE EAGLE WORLD by Sigmund A. Lavine
WONDERS OF THE FLY WORLD by Sigmund A. Lavine
WONDERS OF FROGS AND TOADS by Wyatt Blassingame
WONDERS OF GEESE AND SWANS by Thomas D. Fegely
WONDERS OF GEMS by Richard M. Pearl
WONDERS OF GRAVITY by Rocco Feravolo
WONDERS OF THE HAWK WORLD by Sigmund A. Lavine
WONDERS OF HERBS by Sigmund A. Lavine
WONDERS OF HUMMINGBIRDS by Hilda Simon
WONDERS OF THE KELP FOREST by Joseph E. Brown
WONDERS OF MATHEMATICS by Rocco Feravolo
WONDERS OF MEASUREMENT by Owen S. Lieberg
WONDERS OF THE MONKEY WORLD by Jacquelyn Berrill
WONDERS OF THE MOSQUITO WORLD by Phil Ault
WONDERS OF THE OWL WORLD by Sigmund A. Lavine
WONDERS OF THE PELICAN WORLD by Joseph J. Cook and Ralph W. Schreiber
WONDERS OF PRAIRIE DOGS by G. Earl Chace
WONDERS OF ROCKS AND MINERALS by Richard M. Pearl
WONDERS OF SAND by Christie McFall
WONDERS OF SEA GULLS by Elizabeth Anne and Ralph W. Schreiber
WONDERS OF SEALS AND SEA LIONS by Joseph E. Brown
WONDERS OF SOUND by Rocco Feravolo
WONDERS OF THE SPIDER WORLD by Sigmund A. Lavine
WONDERS OF SPONGES by Morris K. Jacobson and Rosemary K. Pang
WONDERS OF STONES by Christie McFall
WONDERS OF THE TREE WORLD by Margaret Cosgrove
WONDERS OF THE TURTLE WORLD by Wyatt Blassingame
WONDERS OF WILD DUCKS by Thomas D. Fegely
WONDERS OF THE WOODS AND DESERT AT NIGHT by Jacquelyn Berrill
WONDERS OF THE WORLD OF THE ALBATROSS by Harvey I. and Mildred L. Fisher
WONDERS OF THE WORLD OF BEARS by Bernadine Bailey
WONDERS OF THE WORLD OF HORSES by Sigmund A. Lavine and Brigid Casey
WONDERS OF THE WORLD OF SHELLS by Morris K. Jacobson and William K. Emerson
WONDERS OF THE WORLD OF WOLVES by Jacquelyn Berrill
WONDERS OF YOUR SENSES by Margaret Cosgrove

Wonders of Prairie Dogs

G. Earl Chace

Illustrated with photographs by the author

DODD, MEAD & COMPANY
New York

MANHASSET PUBLIC LIBRARY

Photo Credits: U.S. Fish and Wildlife Service, Conrad Hillman, page 62 and E. R. Kalmbach, pages 19 and 67. All other photographs are by the author.

The drawing on page 33 is by Nancy Winslow Parker.

Copyright © 1976 by G. Earl Chace
All rights reserved
No part of this book may be reproduced in any form without permission in writing from the publisher
Printed in the United States of America

Library of Congress Cataloging in Publication Data

Chace, G   Earl
Wonders of prairie dogs.

Bibliography: p.
Includes index
    SUMMARY: Discusses the prairie dog and its distribution, classification, society, burrow, behavior, and the controversy over its control.
    1. Cynomys ludovicianus—Juvenile literature. 2. Prairie dogs—Juvenile literature. [1. Prairie dogs] I. Title.
QL737.R68C48   599′.3232   76-12510
ISBN 0-396-07366-2

To the late Samuel C. Dunton, staff photographer for the New York Zoological Society for the past forty years. He not only taught me photography and inspired my writing but, above all, was a close friend.

Acknowledgments

No bibliography can adequately give credit to all the help needed and given to me in the acquisition of information concerning this book. The many farmers, ranchers, tourists, and just plain folks who added their opinion and information concerning the pros and cons of prairie dogs—good, bad, or indifferent—are hereby given my profound thanks. Conrad Hillman of the Fish and Wildlife Service of the Department of the Interior gave both his time, talents, and information from a scientist's point of view, and Jack McCulloh of the South Dakota Stockgrowers Association was kind enough to present the agriculturist's viewpoint. To them I owe a special thanks.

Contents

1. An Original American, the Prairie Dog 11
2. The Prairie Dog Is Not a Dog 18
3. A Little Home under the Prairie 28
4. A Complex Prairie Society 39
5. Young Prairie Dogs 47
6. Neighbors, Friendly and Otherwise 54
7. A Questionable Future 64
   Bibliography 73
   Index 75

A prairie dog town

1
An Original American, the Prairie Dog

A brown, furry little animal, about 2 pounds in weight and only 15 inches long, has sat up, wagged its tail, and barked its way into the hearts of modern Americans. A few years ago, this same animal literally ate its way into a war with the western farmers, cattlemen, and the Department of Agriculture's Biological Survey. Many years before, these animals amazed the first white explorers of this continent with the immensity of the towns in which they lived and by the great numbers of individuals that inhabited these towns. Thousands of years before, the animal, commonly known today as the prairie dog, apparently began its life somewhere on the continent of North America.

Prairie dogs are related to the squirrel, although many of the names given to it refer to a dog. The French explorers called it *petit chien*, or little dog. The French Canadians labeled it *prairie du chien*, or dog of the prairie. Some Kansas Indians called it *wishtonwish*. Other people variously refer to it as the prairie rat, prairie squirrel, barking squirrel, or as the Sioux Indians call it, *pispiza* or *pinspinza*. In 1817 it was placed in the genus *Cynomys*, which still refers to a dog. The word is derived from the Greek, *kynos*, or dog.

Despite their ancestry and relationship to the squirrel, they will undoubtedly always be dogs to casual observers. While watching a colony of them in action, anyone can easily imagine a field of brown puppies running, wrestling, grooming each other, bickering, or touching noses. They even sit up as if begging for a dog biscuit, and their little yelps or barks could be those of your own pup. If anything, the prairie dog wags its tail far more frequently and effectively than any real dog can.

Prairie dogs are members of the order Rodentia, or rodents, and have the four elongated incisor teeth for snipping or gnawing that are characteristic of this order. The rodents are one of the first of the mammals to have evolved, which, according to fossil records, took place about 60 million years ago, near the end of the reign of the giant dinosaurs and the beginning of the flowering plants. Approximately 35 million years later, fossil records show that the rodents divided into several families, and one is named Sciuridae, or the squirrels. The order Rodentia and the family Sciuridae are represented all over the world, but evidence of one division of the squirrel family, discovered amidst the fossils of North America, was of the genus *Cynomys*. This was our own little prairie dog, and no records exist of its ever having been found on any other continent. Until some fossils are excavated elsewhere to refute present knowledge, the prairie dog must be considered to be one of the original Americans.

It is difficult to say which explorer of North America was the first to have seen the prairie dog, because a number of them

An original American, the prairie dog

crossed the prairie biome during their travels. A biome is an area in which the biological conditions of climate, altitude, soil, and terrain are suited only to certain types of animals and plants. Some biomes are small, but the high prairie biome of the prairie dog completely bisects the United States from north to south, and all cross-country explorers had to travel through some portion of it. Most explorers were undoubtedly too impressed with the great masses of buffalo or herds of pronghorn that existed then to bother much with accounts of the little *prairie du chien*. However, François and Louis Vérendrye wrote of them in 1742 when they encountered the dogs while exploring the northern portion of the biome, and Zebulon Pike, for whom Pikes Peak was named, saw prairie dogs in and around Kansas and Colorado. Most early explorers wrote only of the size of the dog towns, claiming that some towns were hundreds of miles in extent and contained millions of inhabitants, rather than describing the individual animals.

The Meriwether Lewis and William Clark expedition of 1804 passed through miles of prairie dog towns while en route to the Pacific. They were not only the first to write a description of the dog itself but also the first to bring back a dog to be studied. They noted the squirrel-like head of their find but retained the name prairie dog. Another hundred years went by before a man named N. Hollister wrote an accurate account of the prairie dog for the Department of Agriculture and noted that there were two species: the black-tailed type that lives at the lower, more open portions of the range, and by far the more predominant, and the white-tailed species, which inhabits higher, more rocky, and more sparse portions of the biome. From 1916, when Hollister published his studies, little or nothing was done concerning the animal, until 1955 when John King published his work on prairie dog behavior. Apparently people thought only

A member of the white-tailed species

of how cute or what a pest it was, rather than what this animal is, and what it does.

The prairie dog is vegetarian and lives on the treeless, short-grass prairie where food is both convenient and plentiful. It is a small and vulnerable animal to predators and likes the open plains and short grass over which it can see for miles and be forewarned against enemies. Such conditions can be found in an area roughly 400 miles wide that extends from southern Canada to northern Mexico, and from the foothills of the Rocky Mountains east to where the tall grasses grow. This high-altitude, short-grass prairie biome is not particularly good for growing crops. The alkaline soil receives only an average of 12 inches of rain annually, and much of this comes down as violent, flood-creating storms or heavy hail. It is known geographically as a semiarid region.

The altitudes of this biome vary from 2,000 feet on the eastern edge to almost 10,000 feet at the edge of the Rockies. Low humidity and high altitude allow considerable fluctuation in temperature. The summer heat can soar to 110 degrees F., and the winter mercury can register as low as —35 degrees F. The biome suffers not only from violent winter blizzards but also from prolonged droughts and fast-moving prairie fires ignited by heat lightning in the summer. All in all, it seems a harsh, inhospitable biome for such a small creature as the prairie dog to exist in, yet it has not only managed to do so for thousands of years but has proliferated astronomically.

The impact made on the biome by prairie dogs can readily be seen. On short-grass prairie where there are no dogs, the hard-packed sod allows few or no seeds of any other plants to germinate. There is only an immense sea of grass, and animals such as the prairie dog and buffalo or cattle that can exist on such a one-plant territory. The dog towns make a distinctive change in this grass sea. Wherever the dog digs and scratches, it bares the soil where weed seeds can obtain a foothold. The new plants attract new plant eaters like insects or cottontail rabbits, and the seeds attract the seed eaters such as the horned lark and meadow mice. Both attract more and different predators like sparrow hawks and burrowing owls. The prairie dog holes provide shelter from both weather and enemies for many creatures that find it difficult or impossible to live on open prairie. In short, wherever prairie dogs establish their town, the monotonous grass biome becomes a busy, lively community.

Regardless of the harsh climate or the constant hunting by some hungry creatures, the dog towns expanded and the numbers of individuals increased from the time they were first described. During the early 1800s prairie dogs were estimated to be in the billions and the dog towns of tremendous size. At least one Texas town was estimated to be 25,000 square miles in area and contained several million inhabitants. Such conditions of the high prairie remained at a status quo until the white man arrived with his plows, his cattle, and his poisons.

The erection of fences contained the cattle but offered no obstacle to the prairie dog. When they went under the fence and ate the grass, the cattle went hungry. Garden crops planted too close to a dog town suffered much the same fate, and both farmer and rancher declared war on the dogs. Few settlers had the money to buy enough expensive gun powder or the time needed for either hunting or trapping the dogs, so they called on the federal government for help. Because the growing population of the eastern states needed more western beef, the Biological Survey began to sell strychnine-soaked grains to the settlers and soon after, about 1920, began to treat public lands with the same and even more deadly poisons. The little prairie dog has no defense at all against these poisons. Dogs were destroyed by the millions, and for a time it looked as if complete extermination was likely. But for several reasons, during

the 1950s the program was slowed down.

First, the great colonies were gone, and second, many ranchers and farmers found they sort of liked and even missed having a few dogs around. They claimed to want and need control, not extermination. Then, the traveling public discovered the prairie dogs in some of the national parks where poisoning was taboo and argued against complete destruction of these cute little animals. Another, and maybe the most important reason for stopping much of the program, was the nonselective nature of the poisons used. Many forms of life other than prairie dogs were being destroyed, some by eating the poison directly and others by secondary poisoning from eating dead animals. Unfortunately, the prolific dogs are once more reaching destructive proportions, and the cry for help is again growing strong.

2

The Prairie Dog Is Not a Dog

The prairie dog is doglike only to the casual observer. An active colony of them might remind the observer of a yard full of puppies, but here the resemblance stops. Dogs belong to the family Canidae, as do wolves and foxes. They are meat eaters that have long legs and canine teeth used for chasing and killing their prey. The prairie dog is quite different. It has short legs, no canine teeth at all, and the largest prey it might chase would be an occasional insect. It is called an herbivore because, except for the occasional insect, its food consists of grasses and weeds. Its teeth and digestive tract are specialized for such a diet.

Prairie dogs are close relatives of the woodchucks and marmots, differing basically by living within an extensive society or colony, whereas the woodchucks and marmots live alone or temporarily in a small family group. The prairie dog is a smaller mammal than its cousins, and unlike the woodchuck and marmot which spend the winter in hibernation, most prairie dogs are active on all but the worst of the winter days.

Black-tailed prairie dogs

There are two species and five subspecies of prairie dogs, but because the black-tailed, *Cynomys ludovicianus*, is the most widely distributed, it's with this species that this book will be mainly concerned. There are minor differences in the habits, foods, and activities of all seven types of prairie dogs. Obviously, the longer days and warmer climate of the Texas and New Mexico areas will support grasses, forbs, and cacti different from those of Montana and North Dakota, and the plant life and weather on the eastern edge of the Rockies at an elevation of 10,000 feet will differ from those on the plains of Kansas which are closer to 3,000 feet.

C. ludovicianus inhabits the lower, open, flat prairie from southern Canada, south through much of Texas. The eastern edge of its range stops where the tall grass prairie starts, just east of central North Dakota, South Dakota, Nebraska, Kansas, Oklahoma, and Texas. It is found as far west as central Montana, Wyoming, Colorado, and New Mexico, stopping where the flatlands end and the foothills of the Rockies begin.

C. l. arizonensis, as its name implies, is a black-tailed subspecies found in a small area touching Arizona, New Mexico, and western Texas.

Cynomys mexicanus is the Mexican prairie dog and is separated from *C. l. arizonensis* by having more black on the tip of its tail.

Cynomys leucurus is the northern white-tailed prairie dog species found in much of mountainous Wyoming, Utah, and Colorado. Its range often combines with the black-tailed's.

Cynomys parvidens is the Utah subspecies of white-tailed dog that is bordering on extinction. It can seldom be found except in a few isolated areas of central Utah, and is now protected.

Cynomys gunnisoni gunnisoni, or the Gunnison's white-tailed subspecies, is also becoming rare in its small area of southern Colorado.

C. g. zuniensis is the southern white-tail. It lives in the higher

A white-tail

portions of southern Colorado, northern Arizona, and New Mexico. It too is becoming scarce.

The spread of civilization and the poisoning campaign have reduced the populations and numbers of the dog towns considerably, but small, often isolated colonies can still be found somewhere within these areas.

Prairie dogs are small animals. Male adults weigh from 2½ to 3 pounds, the female tends to weigh slightly less. The animals' length varies from fourteen to seventeen inches and they wag about three inches of tail, which is tipped with either black or white, depending upon the species. Their entire body is covered with coarse short hairs which should be a grayish brown color on the back and lighter underneath, but often reflects the color of the soil in which they have been digging. Some North Dakota specimens are almost black from tunneling into the coal or lig-

Small chunks of bread seem to please this nursing female.

nite beds that lie just beneath the surface. Surrounding the Black Hills of South Dakota are areas of red clay that give the local tunnelers a reddish shade. White or albino dogs have occasionally been seen in several areas. Another slight variation in color is due to the spring and fall molts. In the winter months the hair is thicker, longer, and some grayer, but all this is lost when the spring shedding season arrives, and the longer, grayer hairs fall out. Both molts are gradual changes and, oddly enough, in the spring the change progresses from nose to tail, and in the fall this direction is reversed.

Except for during the nursing season, it is difficult for the average person to tell a male from a female. They are look-alikes. When the young are suckling in the spring and early summer, however, the eight to ten swollen mammary glands of the female are quite apparent.

Although a member of the squirrel family, the *prairie du chien* does not have the prominent ears the tree squirrels possess. Possibly to make it easier when diving hurriedly into its burrow, the prairie dog has small ears which are low down on the sides of the head. Its eyes are located high and forward on the head, so that when a prairie dog sits up it can readily see an approaching enemy, whether it comes from either side, directly from the front, or even if flying overhead. The location of the eyes is not its only adaptation to survival on the high plains. The hazel or brown coloring of the iris blocks out some of the ultraviolet rays. This aids vision in a high-altitude biome of intense sunlight and little or no shade.

Prairie dog legs are not made for long-distance running. They are far too short to carry the fat little animal very far at what might be termed a safe speed. For short distances, the dog does quite well, so stays as close as possible to a safe hole at all times. The legs are powerful. They have to be, to enable the dog to dig holes. The front feet and five clawed toes are not only powerful enough to tear up the hard-packed prairie sod and soil, but also flexible enough to hold daintily the thin stem of a prairie plant while the owner sits up and nibbles the top.

The members of the Sciuridae, or squirrel family, may not all look alike or even act alike, but all have hairy or bushy tails, whereas other rodents, like members of the rat or beaver families, have scaly tails. All rodents, however, have the same type

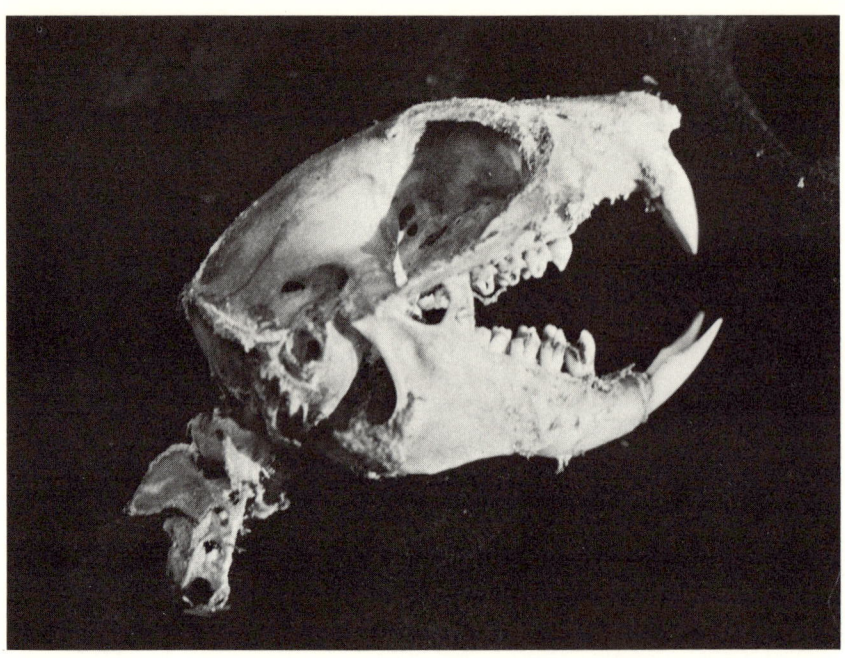

The skull of a black-tailed prairie dog, showing the incisor teeth common to all rodents

of teeth. The two long, curved, incisor teeth on the front of the lower jaw rise and just touch two similar teeth on the front of the upper jaw. These are the gnawing, snipping, or cutting teeth that function much the same as the closing blades of a pair of scissors. All four incisors grow continuously but, unlike scissor blades, are self-sharpening. The inner, soft dentine of these teeth is worn away rapidly, but the hard, outer enamel better withstands contact. The effect of this unequal wear keeps sharp edges at the cutting surfaces. The one drawback is the continuous growth of these incisors. Should the animal not use them enough to wear them down, they may grow too long to meet or function properly and the owner could face starvation.

In either jaw, just behind the incisor teeth, there is an empty or toothless space where most animals have either canines or premolars. The dogs take advantage of this opening when filling their mouths with grasses to be used as nesting materials, and they carry considerable amounts tucked behind the long incisors. A dog running with great tufts of grass sticking out of either side of its mouth gives one the impression it is wearing an oversized moustache. Behind these open spaces are the flat, grinding teeth or molars that reduce rough vegetation to a pulp. Inside each cheek, the prairie dog has pouches into which it can tuck seeds or other small tidbits of food. These are handy when the dog must travel too far for safety. It can quickly stuff the cheek pouches, return to a safer area near its hole, and eat the contents at leisure.

The basic food of the prairie dog is grass, such as the short-stemmed buffalo grass and the blue grama grass that grows on the high prairie. Both seeds and plants of dandelions, saltbush, rabbit bush, tumbleweeds, and many other of the broad-leaved weeds that the biologists call forbs form a regular portion of their diet. Cacti, more common in the southern parts of the biome, are eaten, not only for food but also as a water supply when the other plants and grasses have dried up due to lack of rain. In severe droughts, the dogs frequently dig up and chew the moist roots of all plants. To obtain proteins, which all animals need but which are lacking in many plants, the prairie dog eats a few insects such as grasshoppers and cutworms.

Because plants have a limited supply of chemicals and a low concentration of food or energy, the plant eaters or herbivores, like cows, sheep, and prairie dogs, must eat continually to gain enough energy. In order to eat a tremendous amount, they need adequate storage space in their bodies to contain all this material. It has been estimated that the prairie dog eats over twice its own weight each month, or approximately seven pounds of vegetation. To hold all this food, the animal has a relatively large stomach, plus another chamber called the caecum, which

holds even more than the stomach. Another problem faced by plant eaters is that much of the plant life is composed of a nondigestible compound named cellulose. Most plant eaters, including prairie dogs, cannot use unassisted much of what they eat. Therefore, they have bacteria and protozoans living within their digestive tracts that chemically alter the cellulose to a form which they can use.

During the extended droughts that ravage the high plains from time to time, the grasses and forbs become withered and dry. Because prairie dogs obtain most of their liquids from the succulent plants they eat, they begin to suffer from the lack of both food and water. It is now that they nibble at the cactus pads, which are often the only moisture-containing plants left on the prairie, or dig up the sod to chew on the moist roots of the grasses and forbs. Winter also places limitations on food and water. Members of the black-tailed species do not hibernate, nor do they seem to have the foresight to store food in their burrows. When it becomes too cold to leave the burrows, or when all the food plants are covered with snow, the prairie dogs are forced to eat their own scats, or fecal material, to prevent starvation. Prairie dog scats are inch-long pellets which contain enough plant fibers to serve as an emergency food. During a long dry season, when even the plant roots cannot provide enough moisture for the dogs, they actually manufacture water within their bodies. This is done by a chemical process that changes the stored body fat into several other substances, one of which is water. Because of how this water is made, it is called metabolic water.

White-tailed prairie dogs are a bit smaller, and these do hibernate most of the winter. They have to; their domain, on the highest portions of the range, suffers from longer, colder, and much more severe conditions. Like the black-tailed species, they try to fatten up during the fall months so they can live on this fat as long as necessary throughout the winter.

3

A Little Home under the Prairie

Life on the high prairie is not always easy. Violent summer storms with heavy hail and strong, chilling winds can kill any exposed animal. Blizzards, subzero temperatures, or merely a heavy blanket of snow can also destroy creatures that do not find shelter. To escape such weather, and also to hide from the hungry coyote, eagle, and other predators, the prairie dog digs its home under the prairie. The burrows may vary in depth, length, or even in the number of rooms dug. All burrows, however, are basically the same.

A prairie dog town must not just be close to its food supply, but surrounded by it. Due to its fat body and short legs, the *petit chien* cannot compete with the speed of a diving hawk or an attacking coyote. Each little dog needs to be able to pop into its safe hole with only a short dash. The location must also be where the digging is easy. Too sandy a soil can cave in. If the ground water level is near the surface, the dogs cannot dig deep enough to make an ideal home, and too many rocks make digging hard or impractical. A further restriction is the amount of seasonal rainfall. Too much rain produces a moist, crumbly soil which is prone to collapse, or at best, be uncomfortable. The home builders shun low, flat places that are closely surrounded by hills from which water runoff could flood their homes. Neither do they care to dig on a high slope where heavy rains could rush down and wash out the home. Besides, steep slopes are usually rocky, both on and under the surface.

The high prairie—its great expanse of grass, its gentle, rolling land, and its soft, dry, alluvial or rock free soil that has been washed down from the hills and mountains for thousands of years and deposited over much of this biome—offers all the things the dogs seem to need. Most towns are located where the slope is between 2 and 5 percent. However, in moist years, when nearby slopes have good grass cover, some dogs will dig temporary homes in areas with up to 15 percent incline. These homes are usually abandoned during the winter or when the grass becomes inadequate.

The actual digging of a prairie dog home is an interesting thing to watch. When work is begun just inside the entrance,

Digging a home under the prairie

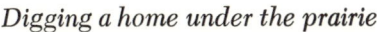

there will be small dust clouds, showers of soil and pebbles, and an extremely active tail and rump sticking out of the hole. The excavator works for a minute, then backs out to survey the immediate area. Whether looking for enemies or applause is hard to say—the expression and stance could expect either. Perhaps it is merely resting. When the dog is digging deep within the hole, the soil does not fly but is pushed out with folded forelegs.

This excavated soil, although thrown or pushed out unceremoniously, is not scattered over the prairie, but is carefully scratched back into a circular pile that surrounds the opening. For as long as the burrow is occupied, soil brought up from further digging is added to this mound, and after each rain, as soon as the soil dries to the proper consistency, it is tamped into shape and place with the nose and forehead of the prairie dog. Little nose prints around the top of the mound are often quite apparent.

The mound prevents melt water or heavy rain from running down the hole.

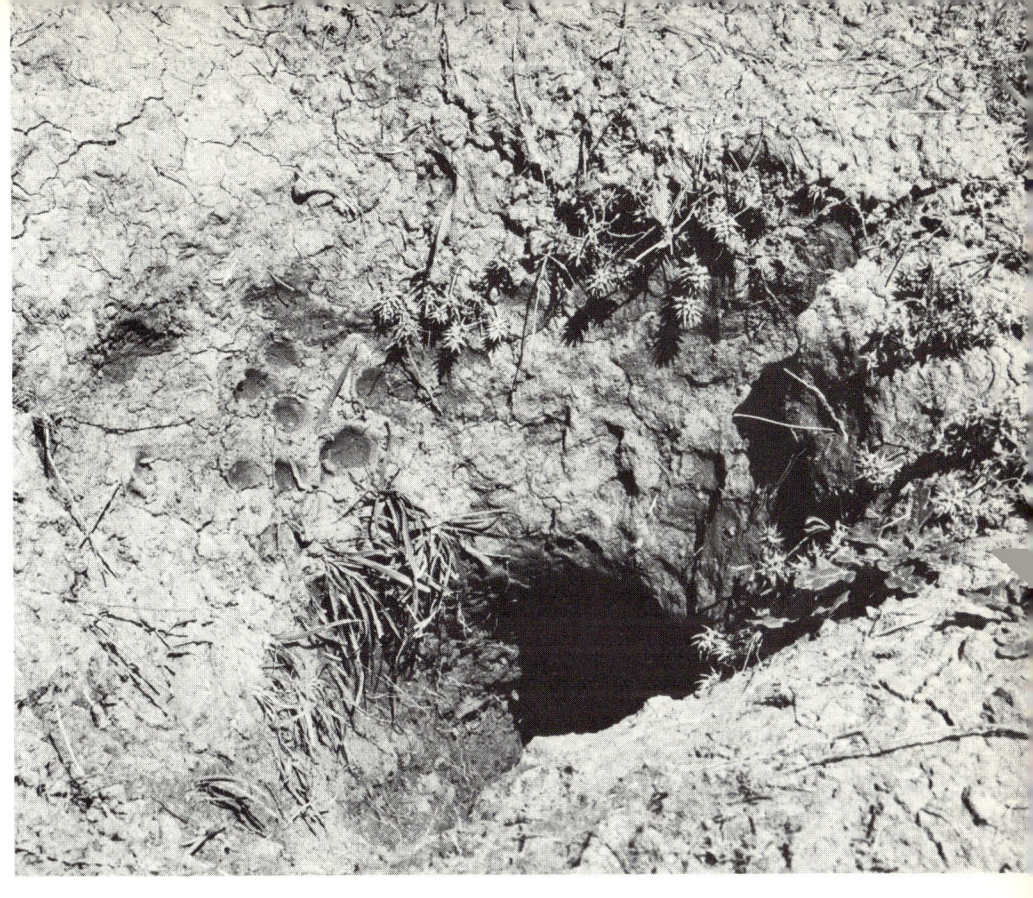

A well-tamped mound surrounding the entrance hole

Such prairie dog mounds are of considerable importance to the builders. It takes a substantial flood for water to pour down the hole. Some mounds will be 3 feet higher than the grass level and up to 20 feet in diameter. Other mounds may be in the early stages of creation and barely existing. An average mound would be about 10 feet across and 2 feet high. Mounds are useful as sun porches, and the owners are often seen sprawled over the bare soil absorbing the warmth of the sun. Another much used purpose is that of an observation post. Any typical dog town has a few dogs sitting on top of their mound looking around. After digging a safe hole and constructing a mound, the dog trims down all the surrounding taller grasses

31

and weeds. This 8- to 10-yard circle of 2- or 3-inch-high grass provides a safe margin of visibility for spotting approaching enemies.

When prairie dogs wander off from the main dog town and establish their homes in new territory, they tend to spread out and dig their holes 40 to 50 yards from their nearest neighbor. As the population grows, and provided there is plenty of grass and weeds, new holes are dug in between the original homes. The new territory, therefore, may jump from six to eight mounds per acre up to fifteen to twenty mounds. If there is still enough food, all the dogs will stay, and when the young grow up, they might dig even more homes within the same territory. This crowding will continue until the food supply becomes short and some dogs are forced to move, leaving empty burrows.

A dry spell drastically reduces the food supply and usually many dogs leave, but when the rains return and grass and weeds grow again, the empty burrows are claimed by new dogs, normally the young of the few adults that remained. The average number of occupied burrows of any area changes continually with the amount of available food. The greatest number of occupied burrows per acre might be seen in our national parks. Here, where protected towns line the highways, the tourists usually stop and feed the cute little *pispiza*, although signs strictly prohibit this. As a result, such towns are terribly crowded, with holes only 5 to 7 feet apart. Unfortunately, in the fall when the tourists no longer come, all these animals must try to exist on natural grasses and weeds adjacent to their homes. It cannot be done. By spring, many animals have succumbed to starvation.

All completed homes under the prairie have several chambers branching from the main tunnel, which are used for specific

A typical burrow: a. emergency exit, b. chamber or nursery, c. toilet, d. listening post, e. mound, f. flood control room.

purposes. The depth to which these tunnels go and the number of second exits vary with the owner and the age of the home. Most burrows have a chamber for birth and nursing the young, another for spending nights and the cold days of winter, a toilet, a listening post, and finally an air chamber to be used during a possible flood. Some holes go straight down into the soil for about 4 feet, then slant off for some distance, and finally level out and possibly continue on for as long as 60 or more feet. Others begin a slanting direction right from the surface, and the entire abode is little more than 20 feet long. The prairie dog holes are home to all the members of a coterie, or family unit, except during the few weeks when the females are carrying or nursing their young. At such times the females vigorously defend their burrows from all.

One might say that the main purpose of the hole is protection from enemies, so the tunnel is usually about 4½ inches in diameter. This is sufficient to allow the prairie dog to pop in at full speed, but too small to allow larger enemies to follow. This diameter, however, does not allow the owner to turn around readily, so it digs a small chamber off to one side, anywhere from 3 to 6 feet down the main shaft, in which it can turn around. It is called the listening post, and the dog can turn around, rest, or merely stop here and listen. If the pursuing creature tries to dig it out, the dog can go deeper. If the warning barks of other dogs have ceased, and the "all clear" sounded, it means the enemy has left and the dog can return to the surface.

A second necessity for digging a subterranean home is to protect the little animal from winter's numbing cold and fearful blizzards. Although never hibernating over the winter, the black-tailed species must spend the coldest and most violent days under the ground. Soil is an excellent insulator against the cold, and the deeper the tunnel, the more insulation. For this reason, most holes extend about 10 to 14 feet down to where the temperatures will be moderate regardless of the surface conditions.

The high prairie is a semiarid region, but the rains that do fall are sometimes excessively heavy, and the resulting torrents rush down the rolling countryside, flooding prairie dog towns and even washing away some of the mounds. In an attempt to survive this possibility, many prairie dogs build a flood control system within their burrow. This consists of a slanting shaft, starting from near the bottom of the main tunnel and sloping to a chamber about 3 feet from the surface of the prairie. When water pours down the surface hole and starts to fill up the burrow, the dogs run up this shaft and stay in the flood chamber. Because it has a dead end, the air in it is trapped and its pressure holds out most of the rising water. Here the dogs can outwait the storm. The water doesn't reach them and they have air to breathe. Hopefully the storm will stop, the water drain out into the soil, and the dogs will be free to either dig out or descend into their home.

Frequently a side tunnel is dug, which the dogs use as a toilet area during inclement weather. However, new or incomplete burrows occasionally show no special chamber, and a section of the main tunnel is used for this purpose. These areas are thoroughly cleaned out when weather permits, and the contents brought to the surface and scattered.

One more room is essential to completing the little home, the nursery. The mother-to-be digs an ample-sized chamber, a foot or more in all directions, and lines it with varying amounts of grasses and weeds. It is here that she gives birth and nurses her young.

Many dogs excavate additional tunnels that lead to the surface some distance from the main entrance. These are often unmarked by the usual conspicuous mound and serve as both emergency exits and entrances. In older towns, the subsoil must be crisscrossed with prairie dog tunnels, and it seems inevitable that they occasionally meet. When this happens among friends, they must certainly be used, but as described in the following chapter, members of another coterie are not always considered friends, and when such tunnels meet, they are undoubtedly plugged up. Much of this paragraph is pure conjecture. Excavated prairie dog tunnels have been found to meet with tunnels of another group; some were plugged and some were not. To study the habits of underground creatures is almost impossible.

The white-tailed species of prairie dogs live in less elaborate structures, or dugouts. Living as they do at higher elevations and subjected to more rigorous climate, they hibernate in winter. At higher altitudes, their holes are usually dug through a rockier material and have seldom been excavated for study. Their mounds are nowhere near as carefully constructed as the

The white-tailed dogs live in higher, usually more sparse country and in smaller dog towns.

black-tailed prairie dog mounds. The excavated soil is thrown willy-nilly out the entrance and is neither scratched back into an orderly pile nor tamped for stability and design. One mound observed in Utah was perhaps 12 feet in diameter and 3 feet high. It was extremely rough in outline, looking as though a huge truck had merely dumped its load of soil and rock. Seven holes were scattered over this one mound, with an occasional head or complete dog showing at each hole.

This huge mound in Utah looks like a load of dumped soil. Its entrances serve several white-tails.

The higher, drier, and rougher terrain of the white-tailed dogs makes elaborate mounds less important. The sandy or rocky soils along the eastern edge of the Rockies provide better drainage, so floods are less likely to wash them out. White-tailed dogs even seem to seek areas of more moisture where they can dig their burrows. It is not unusual to see scattered small colonies lining the major highways that crisscross the almost desert conditions that exist in much of their 6,000- to 10,000-foot high territory. Rainwater runs off the hard surface of these roads and concentrates the moisture along their edges, providing the dogs not only with softer soils to dig in but more and better grass and forbs to eat.

4

A Complex Prairie Society

Prairie dogs, ground squirrels, mice, marmots, and rabbits are all small mammals that live on the high prairie biome of the Midwest. They all dig or take advantage of protective holes and all eat vegetation. Yet of all these creatures, only the prairie dog has been able to expand into enormous numbers of individuals. Rabbits have been known to become temporarily numerous enough to create agricultural problems, but their increased population usually triggers an increase in predators that soon brings the rabbits back under control. Prairie dogs seem capable of multiplying tremendously despite predators, much as rabbits did in Australia, where they had few or no predators.

The only great difference in the way of life between the prairie dog and the woodchuck, marmot, and rabbit is the expansion of the dog family unit into a society. The woodchuck is a loner. Individuals wander far afield to start a new homesite. This allows but one pair of eyes and ears to warn of approaching danger. Furthermore, a startled woodchuck runs directly, and

Half in and half out of its burrow, a disturbed prairie dog warns the colony that something is amiss.

silently, for safety which consists of but one or two holes. The prairie dog, on the other hand, seldom travels beyond sight and sound of its neighbors before digging its home, and normally stays well within this area. Not only does this greatly increase the chances of seeing danger, but the first dog to see it, or sense it, "sounds off" or barks an appropriate warning to its neighbor. The timbre, rhythm, and number of barks transmit the degree of emergency. Each dog to hear this call relays it before popping into its or any neighbor's burrow.

Undoubtedly, experience has taught the prairie dogs the degree of danger associated with each visitor. The warning cry is seldom given when the pronghorn or buffalo wanders in or through their town, but the sight of a coyote on the horizon will start an immediate alert. The flight of a magpie over the town is mostly ignored, but the approach of a hawk or eagle will start a general alarm of high intensity that follows the path of the bird.

The first thing noticed when approaching a prairie dog town is the mounds. Second, one sees the *prairie du chien* itself, or hundreds of them. Finally, a steady approach starts a wave of warning barks that radiates out through the town, changing slightly as it fades out in the distance. Each bark, or yelp, is accompanied by a violent jerk of the dog's tail, a motion modified to match the intensity of the sound.

Prairie dogs have behavior patterns to match each change in the warning bark. The dogs in the immediate vicinity, after giving their most profound warning, are now down in their holes and out of sight and sound. A bit farther away one can see only the top of each dog's head, just enough to expose watching hazel eyes. These dogs are also silent. At a slightly greater distance, partially hidden dogs are barking and ready to go all the way down if conditions warrant. Beyond them are more dogs, some sitting up watching, others running toward the nearest burrow entrance, and all of them giving a less vigorous or moderate danger bark.

Looking back when walking through a dog town, one sees the reversal of the pattern. Hidden dogs come up to peek. Peeking

A prairie dog on the alert

dogs assume the crouch and start to bark. Crouching dogs sit up and bark also, and finally, way back, normal activities are resumed. The final act takes place when all danger is passed and some dog, after a long hard look in all directions, sits up and barks the "all clear." This action is often so energetically presented that it upsets the animal and lands it on its back. To do it properly, the dog must sit up as high and straight as possible, lean back a trifle, lift its head another trifle, and emit its longest and loudest bark. The posture, the violent jerk of its tail, and the energy expended require more balance than some younger dogs have.

A prairie dog town is an active place. The little ones are chasing, wrestling, grooming, and frequently hugging and kissing each other. Some adults are sprawled out on their mounds enjoying the sun, others are sitting up, looking over the scene. Each may be eating, either nuzzling the grass for a tidbit or sitting up holding a weed stem in its forefeet while eating the top. A large male can usually be seen walking around the area, stop-

A kiss

ping now and then to kiss and embrace another dog or, as like as not, to crouch down and snarl at it. It's not too unlikely that this larger dog will even engage in a fight or two as it prowls, or at least chase another dog for 20 or 30 feet before it gives up and resumes prowling. All these activities are normal, but it took years of observing the dog town in its entirety and especially marked individuals, before the heart of the dog town could be understood. The heart of the town is called the coterie.

A coterie is the prairie dog equivalent of a small neighborhood. It could be described as an area, along with its inhabitants, that is about one-third of an acre in extent. We can't see it; it is neither fenced nor visually marked, but the owners know its boundaries, and every dog that belongs on it. Woe betide the dog from another coterie who ventures across the line. It is immediately challenged and, if possible, driven off with or without a fight.

Patrol duty. The perimeter of the coterie must be inspected constantly.

Recognition of family members is probably accomplished by both sight and odor, but is usually assured by an open-mouthed kiss. The amount of kissing, hugging, cuddling, and grooming by a family is astonishing. When patrolling the coterie perimeter, should the male encounter another dog which it recognizes, kisses are exchanged. If, however, it is not sure of the dog, it crouches down and snarls. If the stranger is ready for a fight, it snarls back, and the fight might well begin. Sometimes the stranger may merely seek to pass through. Then, instead of snarling, the stranger stands still until its anal glands have been properly sniffed. After passing this inspection, the stranger returns the compliment and continues on its way.

The inhabitants of the coterie vary in number. Usually there is a large dominant male, one or two mature females, and all the offspring of the last year or two. The number in a family varies in relation to the available food. During the years of adequate rainfall, the coterie can support more appetites than a dry year can. When the food supply grows short, some of the dogs leave voluntarily and others may be driven out.

As with man, a prairie dog's home is its castle, and during normal activities, each dog retires to its own or the family's burrow only. During times of danger, when warning barks are sounded, any dog seems to be welcome in the nearest hole. There is little or no aimless running, except for the very young who have not yet learned the exact locations.

A coterie is stable in area, but not in membership. Except for the marginal coteries that ring the dog town, the homestead is hemmed in by the neighbor's property, and must remain the same size. The number of animals, however, is affected by many factors. In the early spring, the soil is moist with both melting snows and spring rains. Grass and forbs are lush and abundant, and the five to eight members of the family unit find ample sus-

A prairie dog at home

tenance, even though they may be exceptionally hungry after a long winter, and the nursing mother may need extra food. Later, if two or more females bring their litters of four to six to the surface to share the same amount of food, some of the members might be forced to move on. Either the yearlings or, in some instances, the original adults move to new locations. A hot, dry summer can wither all the foliage and cause the entire family to move, individually or sometimes collectively. Excessive predation, drowning due to exceptionally heavy or repetitious floods, prairie fires, or even disease can thin out the coterie—or on occasion, an entire town. Prairie dogs are susceptible to sylvatic plague, which is carried by fleas on the dogs, just as it is by the fleas on rats. Counts made of individual dogs per acre vary from forty when moisture and food are excellent to only one or two during prolonged drought.

Dog towns are limited in size and membership by forces like weather, food, flood, or by overpopulation. As the numbers increase, there is bound to be less of the choice foods for each individual. There is also an increase in contact between dogs and a resulting rise in the number of fights over the better grass, or over which dog can sit on the mound and sun itself. In a thinly populated, new coterie under ideal weather conditions, each member can leisurely eat all it needs or wants. The well-fed, presumably comfortable females will produce the maximum number of young each year. As the young grow and demand their share of the limited food within the boundaries, the competition for this food grows also. Eventually there reaches a point where the amount and type of food are inadequate. Food must be fought over, eaten hurriedly, and undoubtedly poorly digested. At this point, it has been discovered that although the older females produce young, there are fewer of them, and many die from malnutrition. The yearling females that normally would bear young do not.

5

Young Prairie Dogs

Observers at a prairie dog town are often heard to comment on the dogs that bear obvious scars on either face or body. As loving and cuddly as prairie dogs seem to be, they are not always that way. Few of these scars are due to predators, but to fighting amongst themselves. Many fights take place at the coterie boundaries where patrolling dogs ward off trespassers. Other fights occur between two males endeavoring to mate with the same female, and last, some scars are received during a rough and tumble fight with a female who was either not ready to mate or else was already impregnated by another male and was vigorously defending her burrow.

Sexual awareness is not a year-round sense in prairie dogs. For a large portion of the year, males and females are not only look-alikes but act-alikes. It is only during a one- to five-week period of each year that the sexual glands of either are active.

Breeding time varies with the geographical location of the dog. In the north on the high plains of the Dakotas, the males

A choice tidbit is nibbled daintily.

begin seeking mates in late February or March, and for four or five weeks are capable of impregnating the females. They, however, receive their sexual impetus later than the males, have a week or so of reproductive capacity, then either become pregnant or lose both interest and ability. On the southern plains, the reproductive activities begin in January, or a month sooner. The biological urge and ability to reproduce are timed so the young reach an age and sufficient strength to come to the surface of the prairie when the new spring grasses are just starting, or about when the outside temperature averages 55 degrees F.

In the fall, all members of a dog town spend most of their daytime hours eating as much as possible. They are building up a good layer of fat in their bodies to aid them in surviving the long winter months when food is scarce and the cold and snowy days prevent them from foraging. A bit later, the males' reproductive glands become active. As the annual breeding season progresses, the males become more and more active, yet pay less attention to feeding. As the glands resume full activity, the males start looking for suitable mates. In their quest, they invade coteries other than their own, provoking battle after battle. They are seen chasing desirable females who run for their burrow, often stopping at the entrance to fight.

Actual mating must take place underground because there is little or no visual knowledge of it, and captive specimens are reluctant to breed under observation. Once gestation has started, the female carries great mouthfuls of grass and hay to the nursery chamber underground and becomes extremely belligerent toward any visitors who may approach her burrow.

Gestation lasts about thirty-two days, and the youngsters are only 2½ inches long, hairless, and under an ounce in weight at birth. For the next six weeks they remain in the nursery with their mother who, when the weather permits, makes foraging trips to the surface for food. They are still nursing, or trying to, when they make their entrance into the world of light, but mother usually gently pushes them away in an attempt to wean them. An average litter is from four to six young for an older female, and three in a litter for a yearling. The maximum litter is ten pups. If food has been scarce or the coterie overpopulated, the yearling females may not produce any young at all and the older female will usually produce but two or three pups.

When the young prairie dogs appear at the surface, they are small replicas of their parents, although only 6 inches or so long. All young mammals are cute, but none more so than these light-

Mother (third from left) tries to keep her young near the burrow entrance for as long as possible.

The young dogs begin to explore.

colored, fuzzy-looking little prairie dogs when they slowly emerge from their subterranean birthplace. Blinking and winking in the unaccustomed light, they look around at the landscape with what must be amazement. In a few days' time, the entire litter and the mother are crowded together at the top of the home mound, which for a while is their security. It isn't long before they begin to explore the mound, and then the grassy areas surrounding it. Within a week or so, these same wobbly little pups are nimbly chasing each other all over the coterie, simulating ferocious battles and rolling over and over while firmly locked in each other's arms—or loving, hugging, and kissing indiscriminately every dog in the coterie. Later they carry their explorations to other mounds and other litters within the coterie. Finally, they even travel to other neighborhoods where their youth protects them. Apparently they have no knowledge of coterie boundaries.

Young dogs must certainly be a nuisance to every adult dog

within reaching distance; the adults tolerate each and every pup that wobbles over to paw, attempt to nurse, or tease into a game. After a reassuring kiss, the adults humor them, engage in a bit of play, a lot of grooming, and rather than bite or shove them away when they grow tired, move away themselves. Young dogs are the darlings of the town.

This is one of the times when prairie dogs are most vulnerable to predators. The young dogs neither know the signals nor where to run. Some, although standing next to a friend's hole, will run a good 20 yards to their own burrow. Mothers stay too long at the surface trying to warn offspring, thereby placing themselves in danger. Eventually, the youngsters learn to duck into the

This mother carefully scans the vicinity for any hint of danger to her young.

Some little dogs cannot wait to leave the mound and sample the surrounding foliage.

nearest hole when the danger signal is sounded. They also learn the locations of all the entrances to the coterie's underground homes and the boundaries of their own coterie. Whether the young learn by mimicking the adults or by being taught is uncertain. Coterie boundaries could be learned the hard way. Each time the partially grown dog crosses one, it probably receives either a harsh reception or a sound trouncing.

Prairie dogs grow fast. Near the end of summer, they are almost the size of the adults, and their appetites have grown with them. If it has been an exceptionally moist year, there could still be sufficient grass for the entire family, and they might spend the winter together. An average year means that the food supply is short, and there will be considerable bickering within the coterie over what is remaining. Eventually, one or more of the family leaves to found a new home where food is ample and conditions peaceful.

Occasionally a dog or two of an extremely adventurous nature will travel far from the colony before beginning to dig a new home. What instigates this travel is not known, but there have been individuals, or even small colonies, discovered as much as 9 miles from any known established towns. Such exploring certainly exposes the prairie dog to considerable danger from predators. Possibly there are many more traveling dogs than realized, but only a few manage to survive to spread the species throughout the prairie biome.

6

Neighbors, Friendly and Otherwise

Different types of food and adequate shelter are the two ingredients that the prairie dog adds to the prairie. In dog towns, the wandering creatures of the prairie can settle down amidst a few acres of plenty. Weeds are a welcome change from a pure grass diet, and they can be found concentrated in relative abundance in the fresh soil brought to the surface. Shelter from enemy attacks or inclement weather is provided in any of the hundreds of holes that dot the town. The holes also provide homes, traps, and winter hibernating dens for much prairie life that is unable to construct or dig its own. Fresh soil and broken sod allow a place for windblown weed seeds to germinate and grow. Grasshoppers and other insects that discover these weeds settle down to eat the foliage. Birds, attracted by the additional insects, stay to prey upon them. Hawks and other predators move in to pray upon the birds. Flowering weeds attract many

This shedding female bison and her calf are probably heading for the nearest dog town, where they can roll and kick up their heels among the dry, earth mounds.

insects, which attract other insect eaters, and seeds attract seed-eating birds, mammals, and insects.

The arrival of the first prairie dog in a new area brings change, and each bit of broken sod, mound of fresh soil, or additional burrow creates and hastens this change, until the mature dog town has made an oasis on the prairie as welcome to prairie life as the palm-lined oasis is to desert creatures.

Buffalo, which once roamed the prairies by the millions, were regular visitors to dog towns. They liked to roll and kick on the fresh soil on the mounds, where the resulting dust aided in ridding them of irritating fleas and lice. The wallows thus created formed small ponds in rainy weather, trapping water which slowly soaked into the ground and gave even more stimulus to growing grasses and forbs. Once thinned out by overhunting,

Pronghorn antelope are constant visitors to dog towns.

the pronghorn antelope are now back in adequate numbers and frequent the dog towns to sample the weeds of their choice. Both cottontail and jackrabbits appreciate the many holes into which they can pop to avoid capture by an enemy. They, too, sample the greater variety of foliage offered by the towns, and some authorities believe they also listen for and react appropriately to the danger signals of their hosts.

Ground squirrels are more plentiful in dog towns. Unlike rabbits, they can dig their own holes, but it's nice to have more, ready-made holes always at hand. They are usually attracted by the concentrations of weed seeds and insects that make up much of their food. Mice are always present on the prairie, but become relatively abundant around dog towns. They eat not only the plant life and the seeds dropped by the birds but also share the insects with the ground squirrels. During hard times, they are known to eat the droppings of the larger animals.

Insect life is not limited to grasshoppers. The flowers attract bees, flower flies, butterflies, and moths. The animal droppings attract flies, which breed in and help clean up both the droppings and any dead animals found in the area. Animal droppings also attract the scarab beetle or tumblebug. Carabid or ground beetles, which as both larva and adult are ferocious predators of other insects, frequent the prairie dog holes or prowl the town in search of food. Insect eaters also include jumping spiders, grass spiders, and wolf spiders, all of which depend upon agility rather than traps to secure their prey. Black widow spiders, on the other hand, are web spinners and frequent the openings to the dog holes where they spin their traps across the opening. An abandoned dog hole can often be determined by the presence of webbing across the entrance. Deeper down, both black and camel crickets can be found, gleaning remnants of weeds or scats.

The most obvious insect neighbors are the harvester ants. Once the dog town is established and the weed seeds abundant,

Harvester ants

the harvester ants move in and construct giant gravel mounds that almost rival the dog mounds in size. The ants harvest seeds for their sustenance, and cover every inch of a wide area surrounding their mound, keeping this area as clean as a well swept sidewalk.

Other small innocuous neighbors are the box and gopher tortoises which pause in their ramblings to take advantage of the holes, either to escape excessive heat or cold or to sample the foliage or any small fruits that might grow in the area. In their migrations from one pond to another, tiger salamanders often stop to spend a day or two in the welcome, cool prairie dog hole. As with all amphibians, their damp skins function as part of their breathing apparatus. Salamanders usually travel at night and, unless they find a cool place by sunrise, they can quickly dry up and perish.

Burrowing owls utilize the vacant holes for raising families or spending the day. They catch and eat both insects and small mammals for their food. They do not share holes with the prairie dog. A hungry owl would undoubtedly try to kill and eat a small dog if the opportunity arose. A burrow occupied by an owl can be recognized by the remnants of previous meals that surround the entrance. Prairie dogs leave nothing other than a few scats, whereas the owls leave regurgitated bones of small animals they have swallowed.

Magpies, meadowlarks, crows, ravens, blackbirds, horned larks, buntings, mourning doves, and many other species of birds are frequent visitors to dog towns. They come to harvest weeds, insects, seeds, and some to scavenge any dead animals that may be found.

There are dangerous visitors too—at least, dangerous to the prairie dogs—some of which find conditions so much to their liking that they stay. Predation is a twenty-four hour, year-round occupation of the meat eaters. Although the prairie dog is, itself, a diurnal creature and does not surface during the night, the rabbits and mice do, and many of the successful hunters such as wild cats are night visitors. The hunters attack from three levels. Some dive from the sky, others approach from the surface, and a few are already down the holes when the unfortunate prey plunges in. The estimated life expectancy of a prairie dog varies from four to ten years. The dogs are not only subjected to violent storms, floods, drought, or occasional grass fires, but are constantly being hunted by every predator in the area. Few probably ever live to be old.

Prowling bull snakes or rattlesnakes are certain to remain in the area once they have smelled the many trails of mice, prairie dogs, rabbits, or ground squirrels. The open sunny prairie is ideal, and the dog holes are perfect, not only for escaping the heat but also deep enough to hibernate in over the winter. In fact, snake hunters do much of their collecting in and around prairie dog towns. Both snakes use the burrows as traps in which

A bull snake entering a prairie dog burrow

they can find the small dogs or any other mammals that might go down the holes for escape.

A myth of long-standing has the burrowing owl, rattlesnake, and prairie dog living in perfect harmony within the same burrow. Studies prove that the mature owl kills and eats smaller rattlers, mature rattlesnakes swallow smaller owls, and both these creatures dine off the smaller prairie dogs. Hardly a harmonious trio!

Such a busy place is certain to attract larger meat-eating animals. Before the white settlers trapped or shot out the great plains grizzly bear, the gray wolf, and the mountain lion, these, along with the Indians and settlers, used to visit the town for a prairie dog dinner whenever larger game was scarce. Although their ranks are thinned, the predators still come in hopes of outwitting the dogs' warning system and catching a meal. Man, too,

Gray wolves

The badger

is still there, but only to keep the dog towns from spreading over his cattle range.

The coyote is a frequent visitor. Being almost omnivorous, or capable of eating about anything, it may prowl around at any time, either day or night. Any dog, rabbit, or mouse that is too far from a hole when the fleet coyote makes its charge becomes a meal. Failing this, the coyote will catch and eat grasshoppers, or even nibble on the fruits of various prairie weeds. Coyotes are adept at capturing both ground squirrels or mice by leaping on them and pinning them down with both front paws. Coyotes are said to lie in wait occasionally, while the slower but more powerful badger digs out a prairie dog. If the dog has a second hole and suddenly pops out to escape, it becomes a meal for the waiting coyote.

Foxes, too, visit dog towns, and by stealth and patience manage to catch an occasional dog, mouse, or rabbit. The badger is

A rare shot of the black-footed ferret

probably the most efficient and powerful digging creature of the plains and will quickly scoop out an enormous hole in its efforts to obtain a prairie dog. With no escape hole, the dog has no chance at all.

If the dog town is located close to the foothills where nearby canyons provide adequate shelters for bobcats, these feline predators often ravage the towns. Working mostly at night, they are more inclined to catch rabbits, although they capture their share of dogs during the early morning or later evening hours.

Large hawks and eagles always have an eye out for a prairie dog that is feeding too far from mound or burrow. By flying fast and low, it can often swoop over a nearby hill and attack with little or no warning. There is no escape from the powerful claws and beak of the raptor. Eagles nesting nearby have raised their young almost exclusively on prairie dog meat.

There is one predator that apparently depends entirely upon prairie dogs for its existence. The black-footed ferret, *Mustela nigripes,* lives within the dog towns, using prairie dog holes as its home, and the bodies of dogs as its food. Although the ferret is a confirmed enemy, there doesn't seem to be much that the prairie dog can do about it. The ferret is a rare animal, possibly the most rare of all the North American mammals and, from what can be found of its history, it has always been rare. Being of small diameter, the ferret could easily follow the chunky prairie dog down its burrow, but for some inexplicable reason, it usually prefers to dig its way down to its prey. Few people have ever seen this ferret, and fewer yet know much about it, but the Fish and Wildlife Service has begun studies to determine whether or not it is completely dependent upon the prairie dog for its existence. Most of these studies are conducted in South Dakota, where an occasional ferret can still be sighted in one or two of the larger dog towns. It is possible that these are the last places in the world where this animal can still be found.

7

A Questionable Future

Only one hundred and fifty years ago the great plains and prairies boasted herds of bison estimated at sixty million head. With them were untold numbers of pronghorn and estimated billions of prairie dogs. All three of these animals were indigenous to the plains and all three were either shot or poisoned, until the bison were almost completely destroyed, the antelope thinned out, and the dog towns greatly reduced. Interested naturalists and scientists made the people of this country aware that the bison were threatened with extinction; steps were then taken to preserve and protect them. The bison, which are now safely ensconced in various national parks, are becoming favored by many ranchers, who raise them either with or in lieu of cattle. Laws have been passed to protect the thinned out herds of antelope, and they have become plentiful in many of their natural habitats. Only the little *pispiza* has yet to gain favor and be properly reinstated in its natural environment. But the prairie dog presents many problems.

For more or less obvious reasons, ranchers are not too enthusiastic about supporting prairie dogs on their property, leastwise, not in extensive towns. The unsightly mounds spotting an otherwise level, grassy area remind the owners of all the grass and hay he will not be able to utilize for his stock. Then too, there is always the possibility of a cow or horse stepping into a hole and breaking its leg. Modern ranching is using more motorized vehicles for tending stock, and the mounds and holes increase the difficulty of driving over the prairie. Badgers are enthusiastic prairie dog predators. They dig enormous holes in their efforts to excavate dinner, adding again to the cattleman's problems. Finally, many observers claim that the fresh soil of prairie dog mounds increases water erosion during the rainy season and wind erosion during the dry season.

According to the defenders of the prairie dog, the holes and mounds are good for the prairie. It has been estimated that the volume of soil removed from an average hole is approximately 4 to 5 cubic feet. With twenty-five mounds per acre, that could mean 3 or 4 tons of new bottom soil brought to the surface with its fresh mineral content and mixed beneficially with the surface soil. The new soil also provides areas where seeds can sprout and new plants can enter the grass biome. The holes dug by prairie dogs allow rainwater and floodwater to penetrate the soil deeper and provide reserve moisture that better resists drought conditions. Each hole accumulates fecal material, nesting material, and often the bodies of the dogs themselves which have died under the ground. All these materials provide moisture-retaining humus and fertilizer to the area. Those holes that are cleaned out and renovated by new tenants have this entire fertile accumulation brought up and deposited on the surface of the land.

The problems of the settlers versus prairie dogs, cattle, and grass, began soon after the Civil War. The Homestead Act of 1862 was a law providing any man with 160 acres of land, and both troops and displaced families of the war-ravaged eastern states took advantage of it. The law required that each homesteader cultivate and live upon his tract for at least fourteen months. As cultivation meant plowing, thousands of acres of the

Two black-tailed dogs on their home mound

prairie were turned over, its native grasses destroyed, and crops planted. Conditions on the high plains were not conducive to such agricultural methods, and gradually the homesteaders sold their claims or turned to cattle raising. The first cattle were branded and allowed to roam free as the buffalo once did. They could readily avoid the dog towns where the grass might be thinned out, and move to higher slopes where the grazing was better. By 1880, the landowners began to fence in their holdings, not only to protect their cattle but to avoid the arduous task of rounding up and separating their branded stock from those of their neighbors. Wells were dug to irrigate certain portions of their range or to provide water for their stock, and the prairie began to take on a new look.

Although irrigation had made a few areas reasonably lush, the winds had stripped other, nonirrigated, plowed tracts of much topsoil. Fences kept the cattle from wandering from an area of little food to one of succulent grass. Heeding the demands for more beef, many new cattlemen overstocked their range when conditions were good, and their cattle faced starvation during a dry spell. Increasing numbers of wells and the demand on streams and lakes for irrigation water slowly lowered the water table until, during drought conditions, some cattle had no water either.

Ranchers and farmers alike now had learned that grass is not an endless product of the soil. Land, good productive land, was no longer free for the taking, and when they rode their fence lines and watched thousands of prairie dogs, not only endangering their animals and themselves with the holes but also eating tons of precious grass, they decided that the prairie dog had to go.

Individual ranchers tried shooting the dogs, but it was time consuming. Each shot sent all the dogs in the area below ground, and considerable time had to elapse before another shot could be made. Traps caught prairie dogs, but each trap had to be emptied constantly and reset. Meanwhile the dogs continued both to eat and reproduce. The stockmen resorted to the use of strychnine-soaked grains, which was both easier and faster and gave them the desired results. Some tried placing carbon-bisulfide-soaked objects down the holes and this worked too, but there were still millions of dogs left and thousands more born each spring. The situation seemed hopeless.

The demand for beef continued. The prairie dogs still encroached on the land, ate the grass that could produce more beef, and the effort to remove the dogs was making little progress. In the early 1900s the stockmen appealed to the federal government and the problem was turned over to the Biological Survey. In the search for more efficient poisons, thallium sulfate was tried first. Then, the most effective of them all, 1080 or sodium fluoroacetate, was spread over the lands. In an effort to prevent recurrence of spreading dog towns, this 1080 was used on public as well as private lands.

In the 1940s, the Biological Survey was disbanded and a new department entitled the U. S. Fish and Wildlife Service under the Department of the Interior, took over the duties. The areas to be treated were so huge that at times airplanes were flown over the dog towns, broadcasting the poison indiscriminately. The size of the problem can better be understood when one realizes that the area involved was a stretch of the United States that approximated 400 miles across and about 2,000 miles long —or close to 800,000 square miles. The efficiency of the work was appalling. Even many of the ranchers, both those of the early days and those of today, insist they want control, not extermination, and gradually this wholesale use of poisons was stopped and poisoning limited to mopping up overlooked, troubled areas.

In an effort to eliminate any repeat of the program, there have been major attempts to study all aspects of the situation. There are, however, many pros and cons and there always will be. The answers are not simple. Beef is still a major agricultural product. It can most economically be produced on the high prairie, as this area is not only unsuitable for other agricultural endeavors but is also rich with grass. Since mass controls have been relaxed, the dogs are making a comeback. Stockmen are once more seeking some form of modest control.

The biologists who are studying the situation are faced with a monumental task. They must evaluate and control an area about one hundred times larger than the combined six New England states, and also develop poisons and methods of using these deadly compounds that will not affect other prairie life. The poisons used thus far are soaked into corn and other grains which are acceptable food, not only to prairie dogs, but also to gophers, squirrels, rabbits, mice, plus many species of seed-eating birds. All these creatures suffer the same fate as the prairie dog. Worse yet, these poisons then work their way up through the food chain and affect creatures higher up.

A badger might catch and eat a prairie dog that has recently eaten poisoned grain. Tests show that usually there is not enough poison in the dog to kill the badger, but after the badger has eaten meat from several such poisoned dogs, the accumulation can cause its death. In the same way, owls, eagles, coyotes, bobcats, hawks, and all forms of carnivorous animals which are high in the food chain can ultimately be poisoned. The same fate awaits all the scavengers, such as vultures, crows, and ravens, which flock to the feast of dead or dying creatures.

An even more frightening possibility would be the effect of rain on the poisoned grains. Some poisons that are water soluble could be splashed onto both grass and weeds that are to be eaten by stock. Other poisons could be carried by rainwater into the soil, washed into streams or ponds, or some could be absorbed by edible prairie plants and gradually work their way up through the food chain where an accumulation could be disastrous. Therefore the biologists must search for a poison or a method that will control prairie dogs only. It must be short-lived or nonresidual, so that its effect lasts just long enough to destroy the prairie dog and not travel up the food chain. It must be reasonable in price and fast in application. The biologists must also try to answer the predatory question in a way satisfactory to all. Some people say that prairie dogs attract and increase the numbers of all types of predators. Others claim that, due to lack of the dogs and their rodent neighbors, farm animals are preyed upon.

Neither farmer, rancher, nor biologist can agree on the answers. There are too many differences in elevation, weather, climate, topography, soil, and even land use over this immense area. This one huge biome is divided into several mini-biomes,

Another kiss

all capable of supporting cattle, sheep, or prairie dogs, but all creating slightly different problems requiring separate answers.

A compassionate, rather than a financial issue, also faces the biologists. What is to be the fate of the black-footed ferret? Does it need the prairie dog for survival? If so, how large a town is necessary for its support, and how many ferrets can exist in one town? Can it be introduced into a protected dog town and survive? The ferret is thought already so rare that a wrong guess could cause its extinction.

The future of the wild prarie dog hangs in limbo. Stockmen and farmers are once more feeling the effects of its rapid reproduction and grass-eating capabilities. They are again practicing individual controls with about the same results their fathers and grandfathers had. Control is necessary, but not the devastating effects of mass poisoning.

There is, however, little or no chance that prairie dogs will be pushed to extinction or even near to it. Too many people like the little *prairie du chien*. Many a farmer and rancher derives as much pleasure from watching the *wishtonwish* down in the south forty as the tourist does in our national parks. Many a town or city within the biome has its acre or two set aside within the city or town limits where the prairie dog lives under complete protection, and with ample food.

National parks located in appropriate areas have some rather sizable dog towns within their boundaries. Wind Cave National Park and Custer State Park of South Dakota, Theodore Roosevelt National Park of North Dakota, Devils Tower National Park in Wyoming, and the Wichita Mountains of Kansas are but a few of them. Even a few smaller private zoos or tourist stops cherish small prairie dog exhibits.

What might be missed are the endless miles of towns and the millions of wild dogs running, barking, wagging their tails, and stretching from horizon to horizon. That's what it was in the old days, but like those old days, the seemingly endless prairie dog towns are gone forever.

Bibliography

Anthony, H. E. 1928. *Field Book of North American Mammals.* New York: Putnam's.

The Audubon Nature Encyclopedia. 1971. Philadelphia and New York: Curtis.

Carrington, Richard. 1963. *Mammals.* Life Nature Library. New York: Time-Life.

Costello, David F. 1970. *The World of the Prairie Dog.* Philadelphia and New York: Lippincott.

Farb, Peter. 1964. *Land and Wildlife of North America.* Life Nature Library. New York: Time-Life.

Koford, Carl. 1958. *Prairie Dogs, Whitefaces and Blue Grama.* A Wildlife Monograph. New York Zoological Society and the Conservation Foundation.

McClung, Robert M. 1969. *Lost Wild America.* New York: Morrow.

McNulty, Faith. 1971. *Must They Die?* Garden City, N.Y.: Doubleday.

Orr, Robert T. 1971. *Mammals of North America*. Garden City, N.Y.: Doubleday.

Romer, Alfred S. 1933. *Man and the Vertebrates*. Chicago: University of Chicago Press.

Tinbergen, Niko. 1965. *Animal Behavior*. Life Nature Library. New York: Time-Life.

Index

Antelope, pronghorn, 56, 64
Ants, harvester, 57-58

Badgers, 61-62, 66, 70
Bears, grizzly, 60
Beetles, 57
Biome, 13-16, 23, 25, 29, 39, 53, 70, 72
Birds, 58, 62, 70
Bison (buffalo), 55, 64
Black-tailed species, 14, 19, 20, 21, 27, 34, 37
Bobcats, 62, 70
Breeding, 47-48
Burrows, 28-38

Care of young, 49
Cattle, 67
Cellulose, 26
Chambers, 33-36
Classification, 12

Color, 21-23
Coterie, 43-46, 52
Coyotes, 61, 70
Crickets, 57
Cynomys, 12
Cynomys gunnisoni gunnisoni, 20
Cynomys gunnisoni zuniensis, 20
Cynomys leucurus, 20
Cynomys ludovicianus, 19
Cynomys ludovicianus arizonensis, 20
Cynomys mexicanus, 20
Cynomys parvidens, 20

Diet, 18, 25, 54
Digestive system, 25-26

Eagles, 62, 70
Ears, 23
Emergency exits, 33, 36
Eyes, 23

75

Ferrets, black-footed, 62-63, 71
Fighting, 44, 46, 47
Flies, 57
Flood control system, 35
Food, 15, 18, 25-27, 32, 46, 48, 52, 54, 69
Foxes, 61
Future of prairie dogs, 71-72

Gestation, 49

Hair, 21-23
Hawks, 62, 70
Herbivores, 18, 25
Hibernation, 27, 36
Hollister, N., 14
Homestead Act (1862), 66

Insects, 56-57

King, John, 14

Legs, 23
Lewis and Clark expedition, 14
Life expectancy, 59
Listening post, 33, 34
Litters, 49

Mating, 49
Metabolic water, 27
Mice, 56, 59, 61, 69
Mounds, 30-38, 41, 65-66
Mountain lions, 60

Names for prairie dogs, 11-12
Nursery, 33, 34, 36, 49

Owls, 58, 60, 70

Patrolling, 44, 47
Pike, Zebulon, 13

Poisoning, 16-17, 21, 68-70, 71
Populations, prairie dog, 16, 21
Pouches, cheek, 25
Predators, 15, 16, 28, 39, 53, 58-63, 66, 70

Rabbits, 56, 59, 61, 62, 69
Reproduction, 47-49
Rodentia, 12

Salamanders, 58
Scars, 47
Scats, 27
Scavengers, 70
Size of prairie dogs, 11, 18, 21, 27
Snakes, 59-60
Social life, 39-46
Species, 14, 19, 20, 21
Spiders, 57
Squirrels, 11, 12, 56, 59, 61, 69
Subspecies, 19, 20
Sylvatic plague, 46

Tails, 23
Teeth, 12, 18, 24-25
Toilet area, 33, 34, 36
Tortoises, 58
Towns, prairie dog, 11, 13-16, 21, 28-29, 31-33, 37, 41-43, 46, 47, 54, 72
Tunnels, 33-36

Vérendrye, François and Louis, 13

Warning system, 40-42, 45, 52
White-tailed species, 14, 20, 21, 27, 36-38
Wild cats, 59
Wolves, gray, 60

Young, 49-52

76

THE AUTHOR

G. EARL CHACE lives in Rapid City, South Dakota, where he has been Curator of the Black Hills Reptile Gardens for over twenty years. Aside from his work at the Gardens, Mr. Chace is also an instructor on poisonous reptiles, arachnids, and insects for the Emergency Medical Training courses of the South Dakota State Department of Health. He is the author of numerous magazine articles, a weekly nature column for the *Rapid City Journal,* and *Wonders of Rattlesnakes* in this series.